First
Facts®

Life in Ancient Rome

CAPSTONE PRESS
a capstone imprint

the BIG PICTURE

John Malam

First Facts is published by Capstone Press, a Capstone imprint,
151 Good Counsel Drive, P.O. Box 669, Mankato, Minnesota 56002.
www.capstonepub.com

First published in 2010 by A&C Black Publishers Limited, 36 Soho Square, London W1D 3QY
www.acblack.com
Copyright © A&C Black Ltd. 2010

Produced for A&C Black by Calcium. www.calciumcreative.co.uk

042010
005769ACS11

Library of Congress Cataloging-in-Publication Data
Malam, John, 1957–
  Life in ancient Rome / by John Malam.
       p. cm.
  Includes bibliographical references and index.
  ISBN 978-1-4296-5531-6 (library binding)
  ISBN 978-1-4296-5532-3 (paperback)
  1. Rome—Civilization—Juvenile literature. 2. Rome--Social life and
customs—Juvenile literature. I. Title.

DG78.M349 2011
937—dc22   2010019977

Every effort has been made to trace copyright holders and to obtain their permission for use of copyright material.
This book is produced using paper that is made from wood grown in managed, sustainable forests. It is natural,
renewable and recyclable. The logging and manufacturing processes conform to the environmental regulations
of the country of origin.

Acknowledgements

The publishers would like to thank the following for their kind permission to reproduce their photographs:

Cover: Shutterstock: Andrejs Pidjass (front), Stemack (back). **Pages:** Alamy Images: Interfoto 21; Getty Images:
The Bridgeman Art Library 10; Photolibrary: CM Dixon 13, The Print Collector 14; Rex Features: 11r; Shutterstock: Ann
Baldwin 4-5, Michael Coddington 18-19, GrungyBit 20-21, Will Iredale 18, Eric Isselée 19, Gulei Ivan 1, Alexander
Kalina 14-15, Katatonia82 16-17, Georgios Kollidas 15, Luiginifosi.it 6, Mazzzur 10-11, Mountainpix 12-13, Bill Perry
20, Mauro Pezzotta 22-23, Riekephotos 8-9, Route66 16-17, Sootra 2-3, 24, Stemack 4-5, SueC 3, Trucic 6-7,
Keith Wheatley 11l; Wikimedia Commons: 8-9.

Contents

Romans

The ancient Romans lived a long time ago. They were **skilled** people who built great towns.

In the town

Roman towns had streets, houses, and shops. There were lots of places to eat too.

Rough place

Some Roman towns had places where people called **gladiators** fought. Animals were also hunted there. The Romans loved to watch the hunts and fights.

Some gladiators wore helmets when they fought.

Hard hat

Street Life

Roman streets were busy, dirty, and smelly. Many were covered in animal poop too.

Dirty streets

Some streets had **stepping stones**, so people could walk across the street without having to stand in the dirt.

Nighttime knocks

There were no lights along Roman streets, and some were quite narrow. People used to knock into each other when they went out at night!

Heeeave!

Carts pulled by cattle traveled along the streets.

At Home

Rich Romans lived in houses with many rooms. Poor people often lived in only one room.

No room

Poor people lived in big buildings with lots of other people. There was nowhere to cook and no running water.

Nice place!

Toilet time

At home, everyone went to the toilet in **chamber pots**. They were emptied into smelly pits, or even the street!

Rich people lived in big houses, like this one.

Let's Shop

Roman shops sold everything from beautiful fabric to smelly fish sauce.

At the shops

Bread was sold at a **bakery**, and meat at a **butcher shop**. Other shops sold pots, pans, and fabric.

Beautiful jewels were sold in street shops.

Stop—thief!

There were lots of thieves in ancient Roman towns. If a thief was caught, he was sent to work in the **mines**.

Let's Eat

Romans loved to eat. They bought snacks of spicy sausages, cheese pies, and sticky cakes.

Three meals a day

People ate bread and cheese for breakfast. They ate fish and bread at lunch. For dinner, they ate fish, meat, fruit, and vegetables.

Eat up!

Servants waited on Romans at their parties.

Party food

Romans had big parties with lots of food. They ate so much that they were sometimes sick!

Lots of Gods

The Romans believed in gods and goddesses. They built temples for their gods.

Different jobs

Each god had a job to do. Jupiter was in charge of the weather. Neptune ruled the seas and oceans.

Neptune was the god of water.

In charge

Jupiter was the king of the gods. He was married to Juno, the goddess of women and marriage.

Top god

Catch a Show

The Romans liked to watch plays and shows. They were put on in the afternoon and were free to watch.

Like it? Hate it?

If a crowd liked the play, they clapped. When they loved it, they waved **handkerchiefs**. If they hated it, they threw rotten food!

Boooo!

Male actors wore masks with a woman's face to play a female part.

Happy and sad

Roman **actors** wore masks to show if they were happy, sad, or angry in the play.

Game On

On special days, Romans went to watch fights and shows called the games.

Fight, fight, fight

Gladiator fights were held in a big, round building called the Colosseum. Gladiators fought each other to the death.

Gladiators fought with many weapons including swords.

Take that!

Animal hunt

Ancient Romans hunted animals for sport. People came to see all kinds of animals hunted, from lions to giraffes.

Bath Time

Roman towns had **public baths** where people washed. They only had a bath once every nine days. Stinky!

Hot and sweaty

At the baths, Romans took off their clothes and sat in a hot room to make them **sweat**.

Men bathed only with other men at the baths.

Scraping clean

Romans rubbed oil all over their sweaty bodies. They then scraped off the oil and dirt from their skins with a special scraper.

S-c-r-a-p-e!

Glossary

actors people who perform in a play

bakery place where bread and cakes are made

butcher shop place where meat is sold

chamber pots pots people went to the toilet in

fabric material. Clothes are made from fabric.

gladiators people who fought each other in shows

handkerchiefs piece of material used to wipe your nose

mines places where stones and fuels such as coal are dug up

public baths buildings where lots of people washed

servants people who worked for rich Romans

skilled to be very good at something

stepping stones stones people walk on to cross from one side of something to another

sweat moisture that comes out of skin when hot

temples buildings where the gods were thought to live

Further Reading

FactHound offers a safe, fun way to find Internet sites related to this book. All of the sites on FactHound have been researched by our staff.

Here's all you do:

Visit www.facthound.com

FactHound will fetch the best sites for you!

Books

If I were a Kid in Ancient Rome, edited by Lou Waryncia and Ken Sheldon, Cricket Books (2006).

Romans: Dress, Eat, Write, and Play Just Like the Romans (Hands on History) by Fiona Macdonald, Crabtree Publishing Company (2008).

Index